A Note to the Parents & Family

"Doctors Help Baby" is the first book in a series designed to assist parents and family walk your child(ren) through a younger sibling's hospital stay for a Congenital Heart Defect (CHD). Having to watch your new baby go through open heart surgery so young is very difficult for parents to experience. It can be even harder when you have other children. Even though they may be little, they have so many questions and fears, just like you. There are no right or wrong ways to feel as your family walks along side your Heart Warrior through open-heart surgery and the healing journey.

This book is designed to help you navigate the hospital experience with your older children so they can better understand what is happening to their newest sibling and process their emotions. As you share this book with your child about their sibling's specific situation. Encourage them to share how they are feeling about their sibling and all the changes that have occurred within your family.

Other resources can be found at: www.littlehearts.org, www.mendedhearts.org, and www.pted.org

You can also find local CHD support groups in an area near you. Talk to your child's cardiologist about linking you to other parents like yourself.

Dedicated to every sibling who loves someone born with a CHD.

In Memory of Liam, the boy whose life inspired these stories.

Boo-boos hurt and can make us feel sick. Some boo-boos we can see because they are on the outside, like when I scrape my knee and Mommy and Daddy put on a bandaid to make it feel better.

Some boo-boos are on in the inside and we can't see them. Doctors can take pictures to see boo-boos inside our bodies.

Our heart is on the inside of our body and it makes us strong. Baby's heart has a boo-boo and it makes Baby feel sick. Doctors are going to help Baby feel better.

Can you see Baby's heart in this picture?

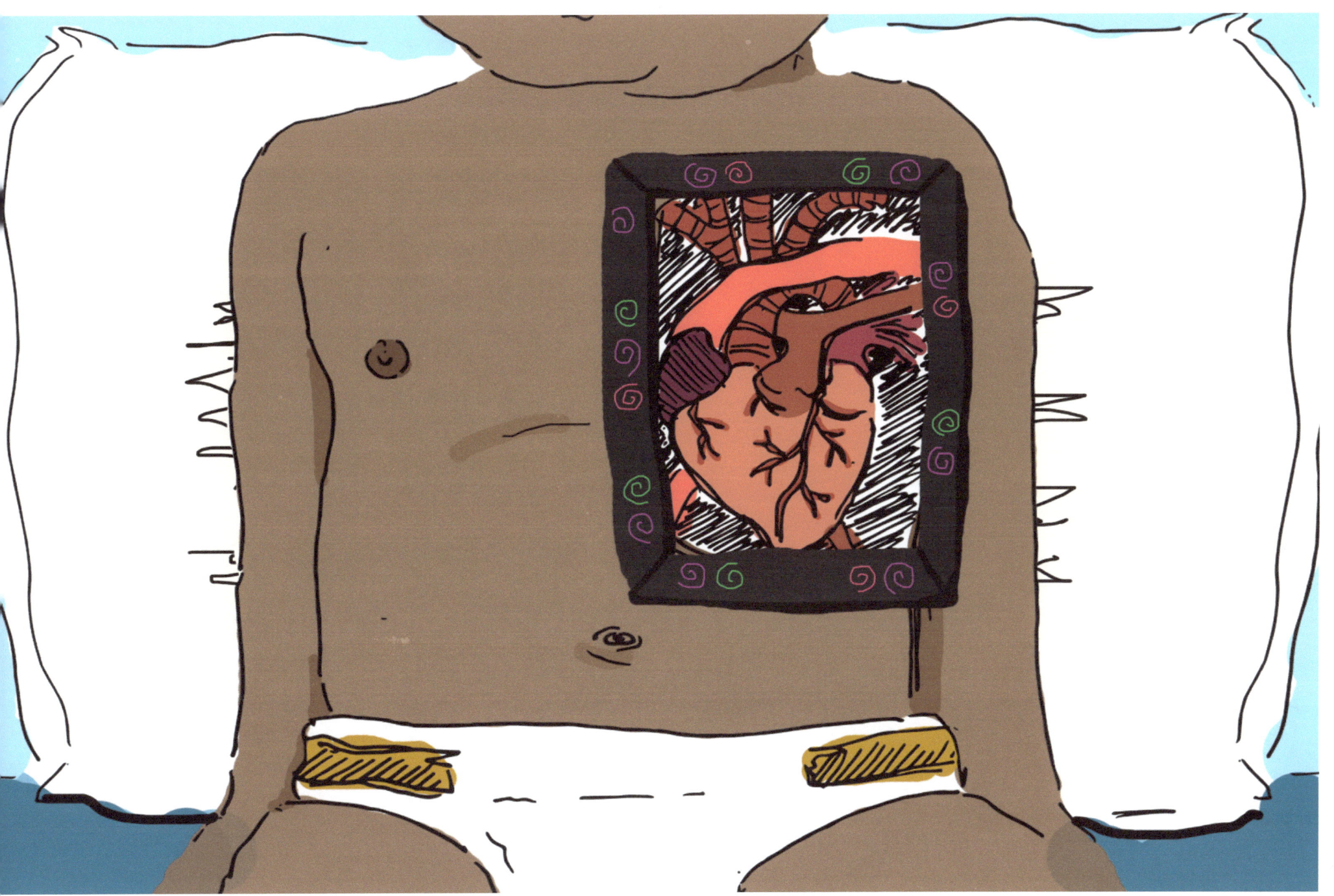

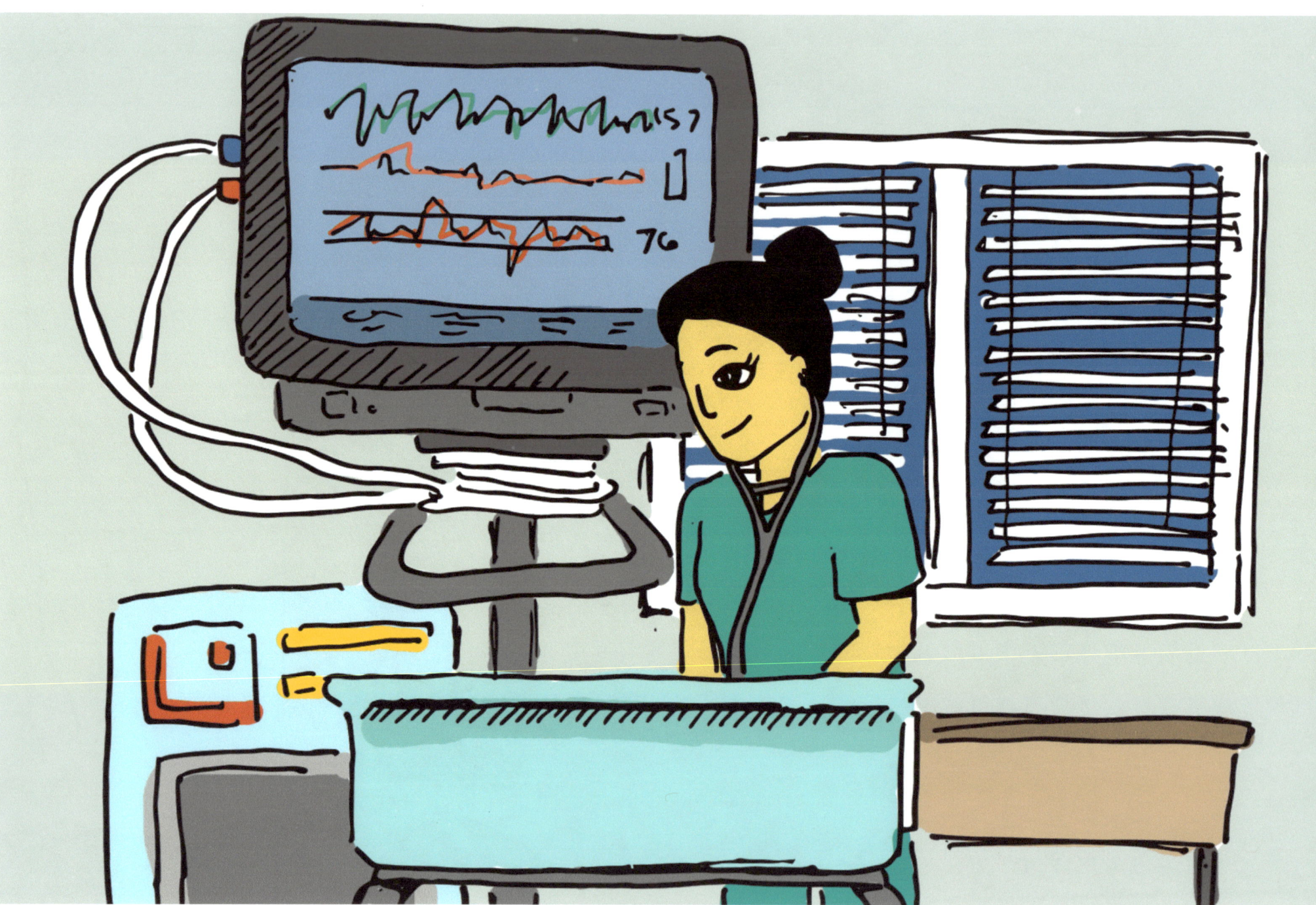

Doctors listen to Baby's heart. They take pictures to see what is making Baby feel sick.

When it is time, the doctors put on special clothes: green pants and shirt, hats, and masks.

Then, they take Baby into a special room to fix what is making Baby feel sick.

It can take a long time to fix Baby's heart.

After Baby's heart is fixed, the doctors bring Baby back to a special hospital room just for Baby.

I am so happy I can visit Baby!

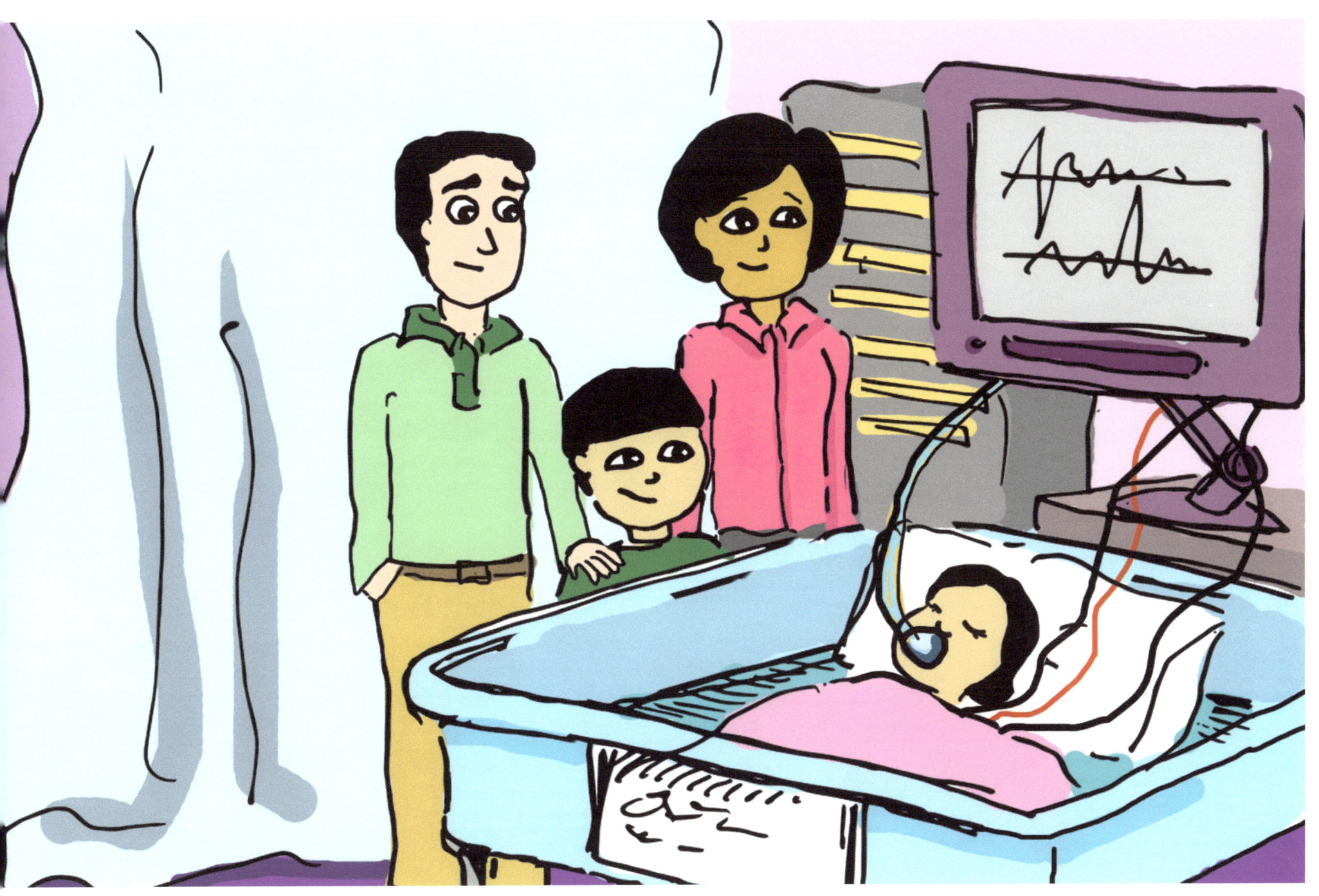

Baby sleeps a lot to feel better. When Baby is awake, I can sing my favorite songs and read stories.

What is your favorite song you like to sing?

What is your favorite book to read?

I go home every night and sleep in my bed. Baby sleeps at the hospital. Doctors and nurses tuck baby in every night just like Mommy and Daddy tuck me in. We both feel safe and loved.

Good night, Baby!

About the Authors

Jenna is a working Heart Mom with a passion for CHD awareness and advocacy following the birth of her son who was diagnosed with Hypoplastic Left Heart Syndrome (HLHS) and who died unexpectedly of heart-related complications in September 2020. She holds a BA in Literature from North Georgia University. In her spare time, she enjoys photography, painting, and reading great science fiction.

Jenna, her husband, and two daughters live in Durham, North Carolina. You can follow their story on her blog: https://heartwarriorparenting.blogspot.com/

Dana is a Licensed Psychologist who feels honored to work with children, adolescents, and adults in Raleigh, NC. She loves being mama to her two sons, daughter, and Old English Sheepdog. In her free time, Dana and her husband like binge watching funny shows on Netflix!

Maggie French is a freelance illustrator and painter living in Savannah, GA. As an illustrator, Maggie does work for a variety of small businesses. Maggie received her BFA in Studio Art from UNC-Chapel Hill. In her free time, Maggie enjoys drawing, cooking, and going on kayak adventures in the marsh around Savannah with her husband, Hansen. To check out more of her work, visit www.maggiebfrench.com

www.ingramcontent.com/pod-product-compliance
Lightning Source LLC
Chambersburg PA
CBHW041324290426

44108CB00005B/127